Indian

ART & CULTURE

Jane Bingham

● Raintree

Chicago, Illinois

For information, address the publisher:
Raintree, 100 N. LaSalle, Suite 1200, Chicago, IL 60602

Printed and bound in China by South China Printing Company

07 06 05
10 9 8 7 6 5 4 3 2 1

Library of Congress Cataloging-in-Publication Data:
Bingham, Jane.
  Indian art and culture / Jane Bingham.
    v. cm. -- (World art and culture)
Includes bibliographical references and index.
Contents: Architecture -- Wall painting and decoration -- Stone carving -- Metalwork and jewelry -- Painting -- Textiles -- Ceramics -- Wood carving -- Music and dancing -- Stories and writing -- Dance, theatre, and cinema.
  ISBN 0-7398-6607-9 (lib. bdg.) — ISBN 1-4109-2106-9 (pbk.)
  1. Arts, Indic--Juvenile literature. [1. Arts, Indic.] I. Title. II. Series.
  NX576.A1B56 2004
  709'.54--dc21
                              2003001956

Acknowledgments
The publishers would like to thank the following for permission to reproduce photographs:
Pp. 5, 26 Jeremy Horner/Panos; pp. 6, 9 Angelo Hornak/Corbis; p. 7 Charles Lenar/Corbis; p. 8 Victoria & Albert Museum/Sally Chappell/Art Archive; pp. 11, 31 Lindsay Hebberd/Corbis; p. 13 Bob Krist/Corbis; p. 13 Bennett Dean/Corbis; pp. 14, 17, 25 Link/Dinodia Picture Agency; p.15 Galen Rowell/Corbis; p. 16 Charles & Josette Lenars/Corbis; p. 18 Archivo Iconografico, S.A./Corbis; p. 19 Alan King/Alamy; p. 21 Musee Guimet, Paris/Dagli Orti/Art Archive; p. 22 Alison Wright/Corbis; pp. 23, 27 Sean Sprague/Panos; p. 24 Stapleton Collection/Corbis; p. 28 Heldur Netocny/Panos; pp. 29, 37 Mark Henley/Panos; p. 32 Robert harding/Alamy; p. 33 Alamy; p. 35 Ric Ergenbright/Corbis; p. 36 Gianni Baldizzone/Corbis; p. 39 Edifice; p. 40 (inset) Lebrecht Collection; p. 41 Michael Freeman/Corbis; p. 42 David Cumming/Eye Ubiquitous/Corbis; p. 43 Sandro Vannini; p. 44 Philadelphia Museum of Art/Corbis; p. 45 Victoria & Albert Museum/Bridgeman Art Library; pp. 46–47 Panos Pictures; p. 48 Getty Images/Hulton; p. 49 Chris Parker/Corbis; p. 50 Jean Louis Nou/AKG; p. 51 Phillips, the International Fine Art Auctioneers, UK/Bridgeman Art Library.

Cover photograph of saris: Lindsay Hebberd/Corbis
Cover photograph of the head of a statue: National Museum of India, New Delhi/Bridgeman Art Library

The publishers would like to thank Dr. Crispin Branfoot and Betty Seid for their assistance in the preparation of this book.

Every effort has been made to contact copyright holders of any material reproduced in this book. Any omissions will be rectified in subsequent printings if notice is given to the publishers.

Some words appear in bold, **like this.** You can find out what they mean by looking in the glossary.

Contents

Introduction

The area that includes the vast country of India and its neighbors—Pakistan, Nepal, Bangladesh, and Sri Lanka—is often called the Indian subcontinent. This area forms a triangle of land, or **peninsula**, that juts out into the sea. Within this peninsula, there are many different landscapes. Stretching across the north are the snow-covered Himalayas, the world's highest mountain range. In the northwest lies the barren Thar Desert, while the great Indus and Ganges Rivers run through flat, fertile lands that are good for growing crops. In the center of India is the high and rocky Deccan Plateau, with wooded hills running along its edges. Southern India and the island of Sri Lanka have tropical forests and long, sandy beaches.

Different ways of life

More than a billion people live in the Indian subcontinent, but their lifestyles vary enormously. In the high Himalayan mountains, farmers live in isolated villages, while herders wander through the Thar Desert with their goats and camels. Farmers grow tea on the hills of southern India, while people on the coast earn their living by fishing. In some heavily forested areas, people still live in groups and have very little contact with the outside world.

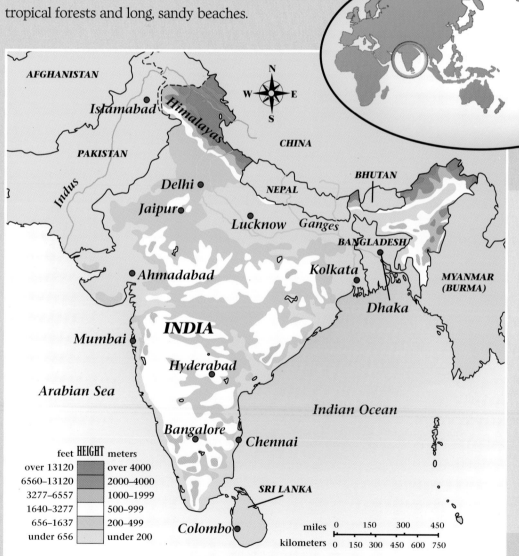

This map of the Indian subcontinent shows the modern borders of India. However, the culture of the Indian subcontinent spreads across contemporary borders and into India's neighboring countries—Pakistan, Nepal, Bangladesh, and Sri Lanka.

feet HEIGHT meters	
over 13120	over 4000
6560–13120	2000–4000
3277–6557	1000–1999
1640–3277	500–999
656–1637	200–499
under 656	under 200

Art is everywhere in India. Here, two women in colorful saris peer through a decorated doorway. One reason for the survival of so many traditional crafts in India is the influence of the great early 20th-century leader, Mahatma Gandhi. He believed passionately that village craftspeople would play a vital part in an independent India (see page 9).

Today, many Indians have moved to the cities, attracted by the hope of jobs, but about three-quarters of India's population still lives in the country. Life in an Indian village continues in much the same way it has for hundreds of years, with people still practicing traditional crafts.

Religions and beliefs

Religion plays a very important part in Indian life. Four major faiths—**Hinduism, Buddhism, Jainism,** and **Sikhism**—all began in India. The Indian subcontinent also has one of the largest **Muslim** populations in the world. Each religion has its own buildings, festivals, and ceremonies, and Indian artists often depict religious figures and stories.

Many forms of art

Everywhere in India, you can see color and pattern, from women dressed in vivid fabrics and delicate jewelry to houses and temples decorated inside and out. Each village has its own craftspeople, and there are many rich traditions of music, poetry, and dance.

This book explores different aspects of Indian art, such as carving, textiles, and metalwork, and looks at individual works within these groupings. By looking at examples from many parts of the subcontinent, it aims to build up a picture of the richness and variety of Indian art.

An ancient civilization

The history of India stretches back over 5,000 years. Farmers began to settle in the fertile Indus Valley before 3500 B.C.E., and they gradually built cities and towns along the river banks. The ancient cities of Harappa and Mohenjo-daro were very well organized, with sewage systems, public baths, and vast storehouses for grain. Each city had its own stone-carvers and potters.

The Aryans arrive

The Indus Valley civilization lasted for over a thousand years, but about 1500 B.C.E. tribes of people called **Aryans** began arriving in northern India. Gradually, they spread out all over the country, bringing a new way of life. The Aryans divided people into different groups according to their jobs. This way of grouping people was known as the caste system, and it still survives in much of India. The Aryans also worshiped many gods and sang hymns to them. Many years later, the hymns were written down in holy books called the Vedas. These volumes formed the basis of the **Hindu** religion, the main faith in India today.

The birth of Buddhism

Ancient India was also the birthplace of the **Buddhist** religion. About 500 B.C.E. an Indian prince named Siddhartha Gautama left his palace and began to live as a holy man. He became known as the Buddha and taught people to give up their possessions and to try to reach a state of peace, known as **nirvana.** Over the next 300 years, Buddhism spread throughout India, but it

This clay model of oxen pulling a water cart was made about 4,000 years ago by potters in the Indus Valley.

| B.C.E. | Before 3500 B.C.E.: farmers settle in the Indus Valley | 2500 B.C.E.: Towns and cities built in the Indus Valley | 1500 B.C.E.: The Aryans arrive in India. Origins of Hinduism develop. |

eventually became more popular in countries farther east. Buddhists believe that you live many lives in different bodies, and **meditation** is central to their religion.

The rise of Jainism

About the same time Buddhism was beginning to develop, another great preacher spread the religion of **Jainism.** The Jains built monasteries and temples all over India, where their religion still has millions of followers. Like Hindus, Jains worship many gods and goddesses. They believe that all violence is wrong and that all forms of life are sacred. For example, they even try to avoid harming insects.

Mauryans and Guptas

About 320 B.C.E. a warrior named Chandragupta Maurya began to build up a large empire. The Mauryan Empire lasted for more than 100 years, and its most famous emperor was Asoka. During his reign, stone domes, called **stupas,** were built at places connected with the Buddha's life.

After the peaceful reign of Asoka, northern India was invaded several times. In 320 C.E. a new family of emperors called the Guptas took control. The Gupta Empire is famous for its beautiful wall paintings and stone carvings. Classical Indian music and dance developed during this time, and the poet and playwright Kalidasa wrote about love and nature.

The graceful Buddhist cave paintings at Ajanta were painted during the Gupta Empire, about the 6th century C.E.

500 B.C.E.: Birth of Buddhism and Jainism

321 B.C.E.: The Mauryan Empire begins

185 B.C.E.: The Mauryan Empire collapses

Sultans and Mughals

During the 700s **Arab** armies from the north began invading India, and some Arabs settled there. Then, in 1206 a Turkish army general named Aibak declared himself Sultan of Delhi after the death of his leader, Muhammad of Ghur. The Sultans ruled northern India for the next 300 years, turning the Delhi region into a **Muslim** country and building forts, towers, and **mosques.**

The Sultanate of northern India came to an end in 1526 when another group of Muslims, the **Mughals,** invaded India. This was the start of the great Mughal Empire, which lasted until 1857. Mughal emperors paid to have beautiful palaces and mosques built. Poets, scholars, artists, and musicians were all welcomed at their courts.

The British in India

From the 1500s onward, European traders flocked to India to buy silk, spices, cotton, and tea. They set up trading stations all over the country. By the 1800s the British East India Company controlled large areas of India. A year after the first Indian War of Independence in 1857, the British government seized control of the country, making India an important part of the British Empire.

The period when the British ruled India is known as the **Raj.** During the Raj, the British built schools, government buildings, churches, and railroads all over India. Many Indians learned English, and British missionaries tried to persuade Indians to become Christians.

This painted wooden carving of an English soldier being eaten by a tiger was made by Indian craftspeople in the 18th century.

| C.E. | 320 C.E.: The Gupta Empire begins | c. 535: The Gupta Empire ends | 711: Arab invasions begin. **Islam** introduced. | c. 866: The Chola kingdom begins | 1206: The Sultanate of Delhi begins |

8

Independence and after

Eventually, the Indian people demanded the right to govern themselves. Following their inspiring leader, Mahatma Gandhi, they campaigned for an end to British rule. Finally, in 1947 India became independent. But India's Muslims and **Hindus** could not agree on their country's future. Consequently, the day before independence, the mainly Muslim areas in the north formed the independent Muslim country of Pakistan, which was made up of two separate areas of land to the east and west of India. In 1971, after many years of war, East Pakistan became the independent country of Bangladesh.

The subcontinent today

Today, parts of the Indian subcontinent suffer from flooding and droughts, some of its cities are very polluted, and many of its people are desperately poor. Despite all these problems, Indian village life continues to be peaceful. Although television and advertising have had an effect on people's lives, the main events of the year are still the sowing and harvesting of crops and the marking of the country's many religious festivals.

From the 800s to the 1500s, powerful Hindu kingdoms flourished in southern India. The Chola kingdom was famous for its bronze statues, such as the one shown here, which depicts the Hindu god Krishna overpowering a snake demon.

1336: The kingdom of Vijayanagar begins

1526: The Mughal Empire begins

1600: The British East India Company is created

1858: The British government takes control of India

1947: Partition and independence. British India splits into independent India and independent Pakistan.

Architecture

India has an astonishing range of buildings, including imposing forts, elaborate **mosques,** and lavish palaces. Many of its greatest buildings are temples, religious structures intended to fill worshipers with awe and wonder. They were often built on a large scale and covered with carvings.

Buddhist stupas

The first great temple builder was the emperor Asoka, who ruled over most of the Indian subcontinent in the 3rd century B.C.E. Asoka built a series of huge stone burial mounds, known as **stupas,** modeled after the tomb of the Buddha. The most famous of these is at Sanchi in Madhya Pradesh. This massive monument is made up of a brick dome, covered in sandstone, and surrounded by a simple wall with four carved gateways. A circular walkway that runs around the dome is used by monks for the sacred act of circumambulation (or "walking around"). At the top of the dome are stone umbrellas meant to represent the heavens. **Buddhist** temple-builders all over India copied this basic shape for their stupas.

Temples at Ellora

Between the 7th and the 10th centuries C.E., a remarkable set of temples was cut out of the steep, stone cliffs at Ellora in Maharashtra. These temples were built by Buddhists, **Hindus,** and **Jains,** and for 200 years all three religions existed there peacefully side by side.

The earliest buildings at Ellora are Buddhist monasteries. Deep inside the cliff, tall stone galleries are filled with rows of pillars, each leading to a statue of the Buddha. These peaceful spaces were some of the last Buddhist monasteries to be built in India, before Hindus drove most of the Buddhists out of the country.

From 800 to 1000, Jain builders and sculptors created beautiful cave temples at Ellora. Elaborate altars were carved out of the cliff face, and pillars were decorated with larger-than-life stone figures. The most spectacular temple at Ellora was built by the Hindus. The colossal Kailasa Temple, started about 760, is the largest stone structure in India. This gigantic open-air sculpture measures 109 feet (33 meters) wide by 164 feet (50 meters) long. The temple is covered with figures and animals and is meant to represent the city of the gods.

This exquisite Jain sculpture from the cave temples at Ellora shows Indrani, queen of the gods, seated on a lion beneath a mango wishing-tree.

Southern temples

The area around the Bay of Bengal has been called the "cradle of **Hindu** architecture." From here, styles of building and sculpture spread out all over India and into Southeast Asia.

During the 7th century C.E., the kings of the Pallava Dynasty built an extraordinary group of temples at Mamallapuram, on the Bay of Bengal. Close to the shore are five surviving rectangular granite **shrines.** Each of the shrines has a domed roof supported by pillars and is intended to represent a chariot of the gods. The stone shrines were probably copied from wooden carts that were used in religious processions.

Also at Mamallapuram is the famous Shore Temple, built on a rocky promontory, a narrow strip of land sticking out into the sea. The temple has a roof shaped like a small pyramid that rises in a series of tiers, growing smaller and smaller until it ends in a miniature dome with a pointed spire, or tapering roof.

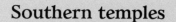

◈ Paradise mountain

The mountain-shaped roofs of Hindu temples are intended to represent the sacred Mount Meru. According to Hindu legends, Mount Meru is a paradise where the gods and goddesses live.

These rock-cut *rathas* (enormous shrines) from Mamallapuram are part of a group of five temples, each named after a brother in the Hindu **epic** poem the ***Mahabharata.*** Each of the *rathas* is carved in a different style.

The spectacular Sri Meenakshi Temple in Madurai, southern India, has five towers, known as *gopuras*. The sides of the *gopuras* are encrusted with thousands of stucco figures from Hindu legends.

Kajuraho

The style of tiered and decorated building developed at Mamallapuram spread across India, growing richer and richer. By the 10th century C.E., Hindu temples became extremely elaborate. The Kandariya Mahadeo Temple at Kajuraho is made up of a cluster of tall, tiered pinnacles, all of them covered in carvings. Inside the temple is an entrance hall, an assembly hall, and a **sanctuary** containing a statue of Nataraja, god of dance. The highest tower houses the sanctuary.

Later temples

By the 17th century, a new style of Hindu temple building had developed in southern India. High, wedge-shaped towers were covered with statues of gods and goddesses, animals, and demons. These statues were made from stucco—a form of plaster that can be carved—and painted in vivid colors. Most Hindu temples in India today are built in this bold and dramatic style.

Mosques and minarets

The arrival of **Muslims** from the north had an enormous impact on India's architecture. In 1199 a Turkish soldier, Aibak, celebrated his victory in northern India by building a **mosque** crowned by a huge **minaret,** or prayer tower. The minaret, which took more than 150 years to build, is taller than 230 feet (70 meters), and for many years was the world's highest single tower. It had decorated balconies and was influenced by the architecture of Persia (present-day Iran).

Aibak was the first in a long line of Sultans of Delhi, and his successors built mosques, forts, palaces, and tombs. Many of these buildings had pointed arches and tall, rounded domes copied from Persian architecture.

Mughal architecture

The **Mughal** emperors ruled from 1526 to 1857, and they left their stamp all over northern India. They built themselves elegant homes with shady courtyards and beautiful gardens based on Persian palaces. The Mughals also built impressive, well-planned forts and spacious mosques with detailed minarets. The greatest of the Mughal builders was an emperor named Shah Jahan, who built the famous Taj Mahal.

Maharajahs' palaces

During the 17th and 18th centuries, the powerful **Hindu** princes of Rajasthan, in northwest India, built splendid palaces. These palaces copied some of the features of Mughal architecture, such as large "audience halls" for receiving guests and shady gardens with pools, but they were decorated in a much more extravagant style. The most elaborate of these palaces was built by **Maharajah** Jai Singh at Amber, in Rajasthan. It contained vast, glittering halls whose marble walls were **inlaid** with jewels and thousands of mirrors.

The glittering Shish Mahal (palace of mirrors) at Amber was built in the 1630s. The whole of the interior is covered with mirror mosaics and marble and decorated with carved and gilded plasterwork.

14

The white marble Taj Mahal is one of the world's most famous sights. Like many Mughal buildings, it is surrounded by beautiful gardens.

City buildings

The buildings in Indian cities are a great mixture of styles, from extravagant Hindu temples and elegant mosques to modern skyscrapers and ramshackle slums. Traces of the British presence still exist in India's cities and towns. Many cities have government buildings, churches, and railroad stations that clearly display the influence of British **Victorian** style.

Twin tombs

The Taj Mahal, carved from white marble, was built by the Mughal emperor Shah Jahan as a massive tomb, or mausoleum, for his beloved wife Mumtaz Mahal. It took more than twenty years to build and was completed in 1643. Shah Jahan planned a second mausoleum for himself made from black marble, but before he could start work on it, his ambitious son seized power and threw his father into prison.

Wall Painting and Decoration

People in India have been painting and decorating the walls of their buildings for thousands of years. Some **murals** painted in temples show scenes of gods and legends, while wall decorations made for village homes tend to be simple but bold.

Paintings at Ajanta

Many early temples contained **frescoes,** but most of them have been lost. However, a stunning series of paintings survive from the 5th century C.E. in the **Buddhist** temple caves of Ajanta in Maharashtra. These skillfully made murals tell the story of the Buddha's many incarnations, or lives. The figures are graceful and realistic, with much delicate detail in their clothing and headdresses.

Painted houses

In many parts of India, people paint the outsides of their houses with traditional patterns and designs. In Orissa, women from the Paraja group paint the walls of their mud-brick homes with bold **geometric** patterns in earth **pigments**— yellow **ocher,** orange ocher, black, and white. In Gujarat, the outer walls of houses are decorated with patterns and symbols to prevent any evil from entering the house and to keep the people inside safe and well.

This painting from Ajanta shows the Buddha, Siddhartha Gautama, before he gave up his life as a prince and became a wandering holy man.

A dramatic painted ceiling in a *bhunga* (a type of house) in Gujarat.

Special occasions

Often, walls are painted at different times of the year to celebrate festivals. These decorations can be simple handprints or elaborate designs. In Orissa, people paint intricate, white lacelike patterns onto the walls of their houses to celebrate the harvest festival.

Houses made from mud need regular resurfacing, and this work is often done at the time of a religious festival. The women of Madhya Pradesh apply a traditional wall decoration called *lipna* between the rice harvest and the planting of wheat, a time of thanksgiving and requests for a fruitful new crop. The decoration is made by first applying a layer of sticky mud and dung, mixed with black clay, and then adding a layer of whitewash. While the whitewash is still wet, finger marks are drawn through it, interweaving vertical, horizontal, diagonal, and wavy lines.

◇ Raised patterns

The walls of traditional *bhunga* houses in Gujarat are decorated inside and out with raised geometric patterns molded from mud and clay. These patterns are sometimes painted in different colors, but they are often simply covered with whitewash. Sometimes, pieces of mirror are set into the designs, which are similar to patterns found in the embroidery of the region. Girls learn the traditional geometric patterns from their mothers, and each pattern has its own name.

17

Stone Carving

The gates of the Great Stupa at Sanchi are covered with incredibly elaborate carvings of people and animals.

As early as 2600 B.C.E., stoneworkers in the Indus Valley were carving large figures and small stone seals. The figures may have represented rulers or gods, while the seals, which were **engraved** with animals and letters, were probably used by merchants to label their goods.

The most famous early stone monuments are the polished sandstone pillars set up by Emperor Asoka in the 3rd century B.C.E. These tall columns had Asoka's laws engraved on them, and most of them were topped with carved animal **capitals**.

Because the animals are carved with great skill and attention to detail, they are remarkably realistic.

Carvings on temples

The tradition of covering temples with carvings began very early. The gates of the **Buddhist stupas** at Sanchi, begun in the 1st century B.C.E., show lively, crowded scenes from the life of the Buddha. This type of carving, when figures emerge from the surface of the stone, is known as **relief.**

By the 5th century C.E., Buddhist, **Jain,** and **Hindu** sculptors were carving relief scenes on the walls of their temples, and they were also making small, freestanding sculptures and towering figures attached to pillars. The Jains were especially famous for their graceful depictions of the human body.

Perhaps the most famous sculptures in India are the figures decorating the Kajuraho temples in Madhya Pradesh. These temples, which were built in the 11th century, are dedicated to the gods Shiva, Vishnu, and Surya. The carvings on their walls show gods and goddesses dancing, kissing, and embracing each other.

Statues of the Buddha

India's stone-carvers have produced many beautiful statues of the Buddha. During the time of the Gupta emperors, Buddhist sculptors at Mathura in Uttar Pradesh created a series of large-scale statues carved from sandstone. They show the Buddha looking serene with a slight smile on his face and his eyes half closed in **meditation.**

Stone carving today

The ancient traditions of stone carving are still continued in India today, as families pass down traditional practices from one generation to the next. Sculptors still make small-scale statues of gods and goddesses, which are used by Indians in their worship and also bought by tourists. Each region has its own different materials, such as soft red sandstone in Rajasthan, polished black stone in Bihar, and granite in Tamil Nadu.

This vast statue of the reclining Buddha is 46 feet (14 meters) long and was carved out of rock in Sri Lanka in the 12th century. The Buddha is often shown with such serene, **stylized** features.

19

Metalwork and Jewelry

India's metalworkers have a vast range of skills. Using iron, brass, copper, and tin, village blacksmiths make tools, pans, and cooking implements. Workers skilled in bronze produce religious statues, while goldsmiths and silversmiths create exquisite jewelry. There is also a long tradition of combining metal with **enamel** to make decorative vases, daggers, and jewelry. This type of metalwork **inlaid** with enamel is known as *bidri*.

Enamelwork

The metalworkers of Jaipur are famous for their *meenakari* work. This is a type of enameling in which patterns are hollowed out of silver or gold, filled with enamel, and then **fired** in a furnace. The patterns usually show flowers and are colored in red, green, and blue. *Meenakari* work is used for earrings and necklaces and also to make decorative boxes and vases.

Statues from bronze

As early as the 2nd millennium B.C.E., people in India knew how to cast objects from bronze, using the demanding lost-wax process (see box below). The earliest known figure in bronze comes from the ancient city of Mohenjo-daro in the Indus Valley and shows a dancing girl. Between the 10th and 13th centuries, metalworkers from the Chola kingdom in southern India produced statues of gods and goddesses in graceful poses. Although their headdresses and clothing are very detailed, the faces of the statues are simple and **stylized**.

 ### The lost-wax process

The lost-wax process is a complicated technique that requires great patience and skill. First, a rough model of the final sculpture is made in clay. This is known as the core. Then, a layer of beeswax is applied over the clay core. The beeswax is carefully molded into shape, and extra strips of decoration are added using a molding stick. When the beeswax model is finished, it is covered with three layers of clay to form an outer mold, with a hole in its base so the wax can run out. The clay mold is then fired, and the wax melts away. Molten (liquid) bronze is poured into the empty mold and left to cool. Once the metal is completely cool, the clay mold is broken open and the metal sculpture can be taken out and polished. Only at this final stage does the sculptor know if the process has been a success.

Statues today

Metalworkers in India today still make statues of gods and goddesses, following rules laid down in religious texts. These texts describe the exact proportions, materials, and techniques for making images. In southern India, bronze statues are believed to absorb the energy of gods and are stored in the inner sanctum (the holiest part) of the temple.

This bronze statue was made in the Chola kingdom. It shows the dance of the Hindu god Shiva Nataraja, known as "the destroyer."

Jewelry

Jewelry is a very important part of Indian dress and culture, and Indian women usually wear more jewelry than Western women. The earliest surviving statues from India show women adorned with necklaces, bracelets, and anklets. In India, jewelry can be a sign of wealth and status, but it can also have symbolic value. For example, some people believe that gold symbolizes life and purity.

Different types

Each part of India has its own style of jewelry. In Jaipur, women wear ornaments set with gemstones, a technique known as *kundan,* while the women of Hyderabad make exquisite pearl jewelry. Orissa is a major center for silver **filigree,** which involves making a lacy **trellis** with twisted silver wire. Rajasthani girls and women wear heavy silver jewelry, while delicate gold necklaces and bracelets are made in the south.

This young bride from the city of Varanasi in northern India is adorned with gold and pearls for her wedding celebration.

Rajasthani women and girls wear masses of heavy silver jewelry as a sign of their wealth and status.

Weddings and wealth

On her wedding day, an Indian woman is adorned in beautiful gold and jewels. Traditionally, the only wealth that a woman has is her jewelry, so a bride will be given many presents of jewels by her family and in-laws before her wedding day.

In Rajasthan, the amount of jewelry a woman wears varies according to her wealth. She may wear a *tikka*, or circular pendant, on her forehead, dangling earrings, a choker around her neck, a nose ring, a belt around her waist, a series of bracelets, and a set of anklets with tiny bells on them. Finally, if she is married, she will also wear *chakti*, or toe rings. Not to be outdone, Rajasthani men also commonly wear chokers, earrings, and bracelets.

Painting

During the 10th century, artists in India began to produce illustrated books—holy texts accompanied by miniature paintings. The first illustrated books were **Buddhist** texts painted on palm leaves and bound between wooden covers. Later, **Jain** artists illustrated their sacred texts with lively scenes. The early Jain painters used mainly red and blue **pigments** highlighted with gold. They often showed their figures in profile (from the side), but with two eyes—the far eye was shown sticking out beyond the figure's nose!

Mughal miniatures

The **Mughal** Empire saw the great age of miniature painting. Emperors commissioned, or paid, artists to paint delightful scenes. Mughal miniatures began as book illustrations, and so they are usually book sized. They are delicately colored and full of detail, and they often show life at court, hunting scenes, and animals. Although the Mughals were **Muslims,** they also encouraged **Hindu** painters, who produced lively illustrations of Hindu legends. Stories of the blue-skinned god, Krishna, were especially popular.

In the 18th century, the Hindu **maharajas** of Rajasthan encouraged the art of miniature painting. Rajasthani paintings tend to be bolder than Mughal miniatures and to use brighter colors.

An 18th-century Mughal miniature showing four women in a garden pavilion. Mughal miniatures are famous for their clear colors and delicate brushwork.

This Tanjore painting of a goddess and her handmaidens shows a typically bold and dramatic style.

 ## Miniature painting

During the Mughal period, artists painted miniatures on paper made from silk, cotton, bamboo, or jute (a plant used for making rope and sacks). After polishing the paper's surface with a ball of agate (a semiprecious stone), they sketched in their design with a fine brush made from squirrel hair. The design was then covered with a thin layer of white, and the artists went over the details with a black line before applying the color. Paints were usually made from **minerals** found in the earth. They included the very rare ultramarine (an intense pure blue) and silver and gold leaf. Last of all, extra details such as faces were painted. For really detailed work, the miniature artists used brushes made from a single baby squirrel hair!

Tanjore paintings

In Tanjore in southern India, artists produce dramatic, glittering paintings of gods and goddesses. Details from the painting, such as headdresses and jewelry, are molded in plaster so that they stand out slightly from its surface. They are then painted with gold and silver leaf and **inlaid** with pieces of colored glass and semiprecious stones. Tanjore painting began in the 18th century, and its artists were influenced by Western styles of art. Artists use vivid, almost luminous colors because their paintings were originally kept inside darkened rooms or temples, where they would need color to help them stand out.

Textiles

People in India have been weaving and decorating cloth for thousands of years. Fragments of printed cloth survive from the ancient city of Mohenjo-daro, providing evidence that Indian cloth makers were using dyes at least 2,000 years before the Europeans did. When European traders arrived in India in the 15th century, they were amazed by the range of dazzling colored cloth that they found there, as well as by the skillful techniques of printing and embroidery used by Indian textile makers.

Many types

Each region of the Indian subcontinent has its own traditions for textile making. In the desert regions of the northwest, women dye cotton brilliant colors and cover it with intricate embroidery. Weavers in Bengal make silks and muslin (a type of soft, filmy cotton). Painted cloth, known as chintz, comes from the east, and Kashmir is famous for its woolen, embroidered shawls.

Using dyes

Until the late 19th century, cloth makers in India dyed their wool, cotton, or silk using natural **pigments** made from **minerals** such as red **ocher** or from plants. The madder plant produced a deep scarlet; indigo made a deep, inky blue; and turmeric created a golden yellow. Today most cloth makers in India use chemical dyes, but they still use traditional colors.

Dyed saris drying in the sun, in Rajasthan.

These embroidered hangings from Rajasthan show the incredible range of colors and patterns produced by the local women. Rajasthani clothing is equally colorful and is often inset with tiny mirrors that sparkle in the sunlight.

Embroideries from Rajasthan

The northwestern state of Rajasthan is famous for its embroidered cloth. Before a young woman gets married, she and her family work for several years to prepare a dowry (gifts for married life) of embroideries that she will take to her new home. The embroidered items include a costume for the bride and groom, hangings for their house, and **trappings** for their animals. All the items are embroidered with traditional patterns and passed down from mother to daughter. The designs often include small, glittering mirrors and are inspired by local plants and animals.

◈ The language of color

Colors often have a special significance in Indian traditional dress. Red symbolizes love, indigo is the color of the gods, and pale blue represents the sky. Saffron, a deep yellow-orange, is the color of the earth and also of poets and yogi (holy men).

Block printing

Block printing is a quick and inexpensive way to decorate cloth. It is often used to make **saris,** *dhotis* (cloths wrapped around the body worn by many Indian men), and floor spreads. Block printers use small wooden blocks with patterns carved on them. The blocks can be used in two ways. Either they are coated with dye and stamped onto a cloth, or they are covered with "resist"—a material such as mud, gum, or wax—that resists the effect of a dye. When the cloth is dyed, the areas covered with resist remain unchanged.

Block-printed cloths have simple, repeated patterns and usually only a few colors. In western India, intricate block-printed **geometric** designs of flowers are common, showing the influence of **Mughal** art.

Tie-dyeing

The tie-dye method of coloring cloth is used in many parts of Asia and Africa, but Indian cloth makers use the technique in a very distinctive way. Indian tie-dye fabrics are usually covered with hundreds of tiny circles of color, produced by tying off very small areas of cloth before it is dyed. These brilliant dots of color are arranged in geometric patterns and can look very dramatic, especially in the combinations of yellow, white, and red often seen in Rajasthan.

This man is using a printing block to decorate cotton cloth. The same pattern is printed many times to create the total design.

Tie-dyed cloth can be produced in huge quantities. Here, mounds of dyed cotton are waiting to be washed.

◈ Tie-dye

Making a tie-dyed fabric with several different colors is a long process.

1. First, the pattern is marked on a cloth with a paint that will later wash out.

2. Then, all the areas to be tied are pinched together and tied tightly with string. The fabric is dyed for the first time, with yellow or another light color, leaving the tied areas white.

3. Once the cloth has been rinsed, squeezed, and dried, it is tied again in a pattern that will later appear as yellow dots. Then it is dyed in a darker color, such as red or green.

4. If other, still darker colors are needed, the cloth is tied a third time to form a pattern of red or green dots. Then it is dyed once more with black, brown, or dark red.

5. After the final dyeing, all the knots are untied and the cloth is washed several times.

Painting on cloth

In the eastern state of Andhra Pradesh, there is a long tradition of cloth painting known as *kalamkari*. These large-scale paintings usually show gods and goddesses or mythical creatures surrounded by a decorative border. Traditionally, textile artists used pens to draw their designs on large sheets of cotton, and they then painted in the colors. The artists used special colors for different characters; gods were blue, women were yellow, and bad characters or demons were red. However, over the last twenty years, the production of most *kalamkari* has been simplified. Fewer colors are used, and the colored areas are printed using blocks, instead of being filled in by hand.

Appliqué

Appliqué is the technique of stitching cut-out designs onto a larger piece of cloth. It is used in western India to make large **canopies,** hangings, and animal **trappings** to be used in celebrations. The art of appliqué was probably introduced into India by Western traders. Appliqué hangings and canopies often show simplified humans and animals, such as elephants and peacocks, surrounded by a patterned border.

Kashmir shawls

Kashmir shawls are woven from very fine wool, which comes from a special type of mountain goat. These goats live in China and Tibet, but their wool is bought by Indian merchants to be woven in Kashmir.

Traditional Kashmir shawls have colorful patterned borders that are woven on a loom. This is very time-consuming work, and today the decoration is usually added by embroiderers. Kashmir shawls were very popular in Europe from the 1800s onward, but by the beginning of the 20th century demand for them had slumped. However, in recent years, shawls called **pashminas** have become fashionable. They are much simpler to make than traditional Kashmir shawls and have helped to revive the weaving industry in Kashmir.

Varanasi brocades

Brocades are rich fabrics woven with warp (lengthways) and weft (widthways) threads of different colors and often of different materials. Varanasi brocades are woven in silk, often decorated with a raised pattern of gold and silver threads, especially on the borders. The Varanasi weavers work on large looms with many strings and need to be extremely skilled to work with the complicated patterns. These specialist workers are not given the usual name of "weavers," but are known as "artists" instead. Their brocades are often made into wedding robes for wealthy brides.

This rich brocade from Varanasi is interwoven with silver threads and has an elaborate pattern of flowers and peacocks.

Ceramics

Throughout the Indian countryside, raw clay and **earthenware** (another name for clay **fired** at a low temperature) play a vital part in everyday life. Houses are made from clay bricks and often covered with tiles made from terra-cotta (an orange-red clay). Grain is stored in large containers made from unfired clay, and cooking stoves are also made from unbaked clay. A whole range of cooking and storage pots is made from earthenware. Clay pots are used to carry water, and cattle are fed and watered from large clay troughs set into the ground. Terra-cotta dishes and offerings play an important part in religious ceremonies.

A Rajasthani woman carries a simple terra-cotta water pot on her head. Unglazed pots like this have been made in India for thousands of years.

An ancient craft

Fragments of pots have been found in India dating back more than 8,000 years. By 2550 B.C.E. skillful potters from the Indus Valley were making pots, bowls, and figures of mother goddesses. They also created a variety of terra-cotta toys, from dolls and animals with moving parts to whistles in the shape of birds.

During the Mauryan Empire, potters made highly polished black pots, while the Gupta period is famous for its bricks, tiles, and pots that were decorated by painting, stamping, and incising (carving) patterns in clay. The **Mughal** emperors introduced a new kind of ceramic ware—urns, plates, and dishes painted with colorful patterns, which were protected by a **glaze.** But these items were made for the court, so the sophisticated style of the Mughal potters did not spread to the villages.

Using pots

Most Indian villagers use simple earthenware pots that have been fired at a low temperature and left unglazed. This kind of earthenware is especially useful for storing water, since it keeps the water cool by allowing some liquid to evaporate (change to vapor) through the sides of the pot. Pots used for eating and storing food are frequently replaced. Containers used for tea, milk, and yogurt are often thrown away and broken after only one use. It is common for all household pottery to be replaced at festivals and at special occasions, such as births, marriages, and deaths.

This fragment of Gupta-period sculpture shows a young couple. It dates from the 4th or 5th century C.E. and was found in Bihar.

 Kachcha and pakka

Clay in its unfired state is called *kachcha,* which means uncooked, or impure. Once it is fired, it becomes *pakka,* which means cooked, or pure. These two words are commonly used by Indians to describe things that are bad or polluted (*kachcha*) or good and well made (*pakka*).

Village potters

Most Indian villages have their own potters who live together away from the center of the village. The potters always come from the same family, and traditional shapes and decorations are passed from one generation of relatives to the next. Each region of India has its own distinctive traditions.

Everyday pots

In Himachal Pradesh, in the high Himalayas, potters make a range of rounded pots and bowls for cooking, storing, and eating food. They also make some special ceremonial dishes to be used for marriages, weddings, and funerals. Most of the pots are made from terra-cotta and are decorated using white and black **slip.** The pots are painted with rippling lines, closely spaced diagonal lines, **geometric** designs, and dots. The designs are often based on animals, leaves, and flowers.

Decorative pots

In the state of Uttar Pradesh, some potters produce elegant vases, incense burners, and plates to be sold in towns. These pots are black and glossy and are **inlaid** with silver designs. After the pots have been shaped, they are coated with a slip made from clay, tree bark, and leaves mixed with soda (a substance with a high sodium content) collected from a local lake—a mixture that turns black when the pot is **fired.** Then the pots are covered with mustard oil and polished with a soft cloth to make them shine. After this, they are ready to be **engraved** with delicate patterns, using a sharp metal spike. Once the pots have been fired, a mixture of lead, zinc, and mercury is pressed by hand into the engraved lines to make the silver designs. The patterns, which often feature flowers, have been the same for hundreds of years and were influenced by **Mughal** art.

 Making pots

To make the rounded pots produced in Himachal Pradesh, potters first use a wheel to make the basic shape. After this, the pot's thick walls are beaten until the pot stretches to almost twice its original size. The potter moistens the clay of the pot and holds a large rounded stone inside it while beating the outside with a curved wooden paddle. Often a pot is beaten three times, each time using a lighter paddle. After they have been decorated, pots are piled up in large, open **kilns** in very large quantities. Sometimes, as many as a thousand pots are fired together.

A village potter at work in Rajasthan. Today most Indian pots are made on a wheel and finished off by hand.

Religious offerings

Many potters in India make terra-cotta objects that **Hindus** give as **votive offerings** to their gods. The offerings are placed in temples and shrines, either to ask the gods for a favor or to give thanks for a blessing. For example, a farmer who hopes his cattle will produce good milk will offer a clay buffalo, while a woman with a bad leg will give a model leg. Votive offerings can take many forms, including animals and human figures, houses, carts, and even musical instruments.

Offerings to Aiyanar

In the southern state of Tamil Nadu, life-sized terra-cotta statues of humans and animals line paths leading to the shrines of the Hindu god Aiyanar. Horses are shown wearing saddles and bridles, ready to carry Aiyanar's spirit soldiers out into the villages at night so that they can protect the people from evil. These elaborate sculptures have been made for hundreds of years. Today, the clay sculptures are often painted in vivid colors.

A potter from Tamil Nadu adds the final details to a set of terra-cotta horses. The horses will be brightly painted and **glazed** before they are **fired** in a **kiln.**

An amazing collection of terra-cotta votive offerings covers the walls of a shrine in northern India.

Plaques from Rajasthan

In the northwestern state of Rajasthan, there is a tradition of making terra-cotta plaques—upright plates that are decorated with painted figures of gods. Once a year during January, Hindus make a **pilgrimage** by bus and on foot, sometimes for hundreds of miles, to the village of Molela to buy these plaques. A priest helps the pilgrims choose the gods appropriate to their own lives and then leads a procession to a nearby river. Here, the gods are worshiped before being taken home and placed in household shrines.

Temples and jhars

The town of Vishnupur in West Bengal is famous for its terra-cotta temples. From the 16th to the 19th century, people built stone temples that were covered with ornate terra-cotta tiles showing scenes from the great Hindu **epic** poems, the **Ramayana** and the **Mahabharata.**

Today's descendants of these artists produce a range of votive objects in clay, including horses, tigers, elephants, and snakes, as well as toys and pots. They also make terra-cotta sculptures known as *jhars* to be placed in shrines. A *jhar* is shaped a little like a miniature bush, decorated with figures of gods. It stands on a circular base, like the stem of a bush in the ground.

Wood Carving

Wood is used in India in the home and in worship. Village woodworkers produce bowls, spoons, chests, trays, and furniture for everyday use. Traditional wood-carvers make religious statues, following instructions laid down hundreds of years ago in holy books. Skilled workers specialize in luxury items, such as carved wooden chests and statuettes, while carpenters build wooden houses with carved door frames, window frames, and balconies.

Different woods

There is a huge variety of wood from which to choose in India. In Kashmir, trays and fruit bowls are made from polished walnut wood. Ebony and rosewood are carved into delicate boxes in Uttar Pradesh. The red sandalwood of Andhra Pradesh is traditionally used to carve figures of gods and dolls, while craftspeople in Orissa make **lacquered** boxes from the stalks of the bamboo plant.

Inlaid wood

Northern India is famous for its chests, trays, and tables made from wood **inlaid** with mother-of-pearl, ivory, tortoiseshell, horn, or silver. The demanding art of inlaying wood was first introduced to India in the 13th century by the Sultans of Delhi, and techniques of inlay were perfected at the court of the **Mughals**. Skilled craftspeople carve intricate patterns into soft wood and then fill these patterns with different materials. Today, the tradition of inlaying wood continues in Gujarat, Rajasthan, and Delhi, but ivory inlay has now been largely replaced by plastic. This change in artists' materials reflects the increased awareness in Indian culture of the need to preserve endangered elephants.

Wooden homes

Carpenters in India build houses in a range of styles. Perhaps the most elaborate wooden buildings in India are the *haveli* houses of Gujarat, with their overhanging, carved balconies and decorated windows and doorways. The elegant *tharavad* homes of Kerala are brilliant pieces of architecture in deep brown teakwood. The woodworkers of Uttar Pradesh are famous for their delicate **fretwork** screens, influenced by Mughal palaces.

Inside many Indian homes are wooden tables, chairs, chests, and beds. These pieces of furniture may be simple and basic, but they can also be very delicately carved. For example, the woodworkers of Jodhpur, in Rajasthan, produce beautifully carved chairs with woven rope seats and exquisite **latticework** on their backrests. In some parts of India, carpenters make full-sized, painted swings to hang from beams inside houses.

This row of wooden mansions in Sidhpur was built by a sect of Shi'a **Muslims** who were prominent in the city between 1539 and 1589 C.E.

◈ Carpenters' chariots

In ancient India, carpenters were highly respected. According to some historical accounts, village carpenters sometimes had their own wooden chariots, which they made themselves, and drove through their villages on them with great pride.

Music

Music plays an important part in Indian life. Ancient hymns are chanted at **Hindu** ceremonies. Traveling musicians wander from village to village, playing tambourines, pipes, drums, and flutes, and singing traditional folk songs. Classical Indian musicians hold concerts in cities and towns. The instruments used by classical and folk musicians are made by skilled craftspeople who follow designs that have stayed the same for hundreds of years.

Classical music

Indian classical music is divided into two main branches: **Hindustani music** in the north and **Karnataka music** in the south. Musicians from the north and south use different musical instruments. Both Hindustani and Karnataka music are based on a combination of *raga*, which means melody, and *taal*, which means rhythm.

Ragas can be sung, or played on a stringed instrument such as the **sitar**. *Taal* is provided by drums.

Musical instruments

The sitar is the most important instrument in Hindustani music. It usually has seven main strings, which run all the way along the instrument, and about ten "sympathetic strings" inside its long, hollow neck. When the main strings are played, the sympathetic strings vibrate as well, creating a rippling sound.

Another stringed instrument, the *veena*, is played by Karnataka musicians. It is made from a hollow bamboo tube with seven strings stretched over it, attached to two hollow gourds. The gourds act as sound boxes, magnifying the sound of the strings.

The veena, one of the country's most ancient stringed instruments, originates from south India.

A sitar player is accompanied by a drummer on a *tabla*. The small drum on the right, known as a *dayan,* plays the higher notes.

Tabla is the name for a pair of hand drums that provide the rhythm in Hindustani classical music. A *tabla* consists of a small right-hand drum, called a *dayan,* and a larger left-hand one, called a *bayan.* The *dayan* produces the higher notes, while the metal *bayan* plays the lower notes.

Both drums have a leather skin stretched over them, held by straps that can be tightened or loosened to alter the sound. Each drum skin has a large black spot made from a mixture of gum, soot, and iron filings. This mixture produces a strong, almost bell-like sound when it is hit.

Dance, Theater, and Film

In India, the ancient art of dancing is closely linked to the **Hindu** religion. There are five main forms of classical dance, and they all tell stories from ancient legends and **epics**. Each dance form comes from a different region and has its own style and costumes.

Bharata Natyam and Kathakali

The oldest form of dance is *Bharata Natyam*, which comes from the southern state of Tamil Nadu. It is described in a text called *Natya Shastra*, which was written between 200 B.C.E. and 200 C.E. *Bharata Natyam* dancers combine strength and grace and use hand gestures to tell a story. The dramatic dance form of *Kathakali* comes from Kerala, also in the south. *Kathakali* dancers wear elaborate costumes and play different characters. Only men can become *Kathakali* dancers. They have to train for many years before they can perform the energetic dances, which often continue through the night.

Changing faces

Kathakali dancers wear dramatic face paint to represent different characters. The color of the paint depends on the character being played. Black is the color for villains and green is for heroes. The paint takes several hours to apply. Finally, small seeds are placed in the dancers' eyes to color the whites of their eyes red.

This Kathakali dancer is playing the part of a hero. Dancers need to be incredibly fit to perform for hours wearing full make-up and heavy headdresses.

Odissi, Manipuri, and Kathak

Odissi is a gentle dance form that began in the temples of Orissa in the east. *Odissi* dancers move gracefully, with small, precise hand gestures. *Manipuri* dancers from the northeast wear brightly colored costumes and perform gentle, swaying movements, creating a hypnotic effect.

Kathak is a **Muslim** dance form from northern India. It began during the **Mughal** Empire, when dancers often performed for rulers in their palaces. *Kathak* dance is fast and exciting, with rapid foot stomping and spins.

Theater

In India's big cities, plays are performed in theaters, but traveling actors visit small towns and villages to stage traditional dramas. Puppet shows are also very popular in the country. The most famous Indian playwright was Kalidasa, who wrote in the late 4th century C.E. to the early 5th century C.E. His plays on the themes of love and magic are still frequently performed today.

Film

The film business is booming in India, with about 800 new films being released every year. Indian films usually have a dramatic story line involving plenty of romance, as well as fighting, singing, and dancing. The main center for Indian filmmaking is based in the city of Mumbai (which used to be called Bombay) and is known as Bollywood.

Like the films they advertise, Indian movie posters are very colorful and dramatic. Bollywood films are now becoming popular outside India.

Stories and Writing

Storytelling is very important in Indian culture. For centuries, folktales and religious legends were passed down from generation to generation, as people memorized stories and told them out loud. The two most famous collections of stories are the long **Hindu** poems, the **Mahabharata** and the **Ramayana**. Written in the ancient language of Sanskrit, these two **epics** tell legends of the Hindu gods and the early history of the Indian people.

The *Mahabharata* was written down about 300 B.C.E. It is set on the Ganges Plains and tells the fortunes of two rival families. The poem contains the *Bhagavad Gita,* or "The Song of God," the most important text in the Hindu religion. The *Ramayana* was written down sometime between the 2nd and 4th century B.C.E. It tells the story of the Hindu god Rama and his wife Sita, who follow the virtuous path through life, known as the *dharma.*

Both the *Mahabharata* and the *Ramayana* have had a major impact on Indian art. Even today, artists paint characters and scenes from the poems, while many Indian films and plays are based on their stories.

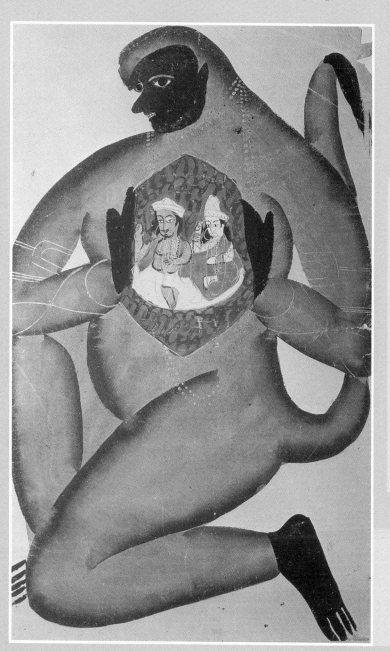

Scrolls

In Bengal, artist-performers known as *patua* make paintings on scrolls and carry them from village to village, telling stories from legends and using the pictures to illustrate their tales. One kind of *patua* painting is complete in all its detail except that the iris (colored central circle) in the figure's eye is missing. When someone dies, the artist visits the dead person's house with a painting that is supposed to represent him. The artist tells the relatives that the dead person's soul is wandering, not knowing where to go. When the artist paints in the iris, the soul can find its way to paradise.

This story painting was made by a member of the *patua* caste about 1880. It shows the "monkey king" Hanuman revealing that the gods Rama and Sita are living in his heart.

This illustration from the Hindu poem the *Ramayana* shows the "monkey king" sending out messengers to search for the goddess Sita. Many Hindu book illustrations use vivid colors and show dramatic landscapes.

Beautiful books

India has a long tradition of beautifully written and illustrated texts. In the 16th century, the **Mughals** introduced the art of calligraphy—very fine writing done with special pens. During the Mughal Empire, **Muslim** scribes used beautiful calligraphy to write out the Qur'an, the holy book of **Islam**. They also wrote chronicles about the lives of the emperors and even created recipe books. At the same time, Hindu artists were producing colorful illustrated books that told the stories of their gods and goddesses.

 Story boxes

Sometimes, stories are told through a series of pictures painted in a story box. The box, known as a *kavad*, is shaped like a human, and so it represents the storyteller. As the story box is opened up, more and more scenes from the story are revealed.

Crafts

The Indian subcontinent is full of craftspeople. Most of them work at home in their villages, but some have small workshops in cities. Families pass on these skills from one generation to the next, keeping the crafts alive in Indian regional cultures.

Leatherwork

Almost every Indian village has a cobbler who makes leather bags, saddles, and sandals known as *chappals*. In the cities, leatherworkers often create more elaborate items, such as pointed slippers with elaborate fabric decorations stitched onto them. Leatherworkers in the Punjab create **appliqué** patterns by stitching colored leather pieces onto an undyed leather base. Skilled craftspeople in Madhya Pradesh embroider red leather with gold and silk thread. In the desert regions of the northwest, lamps and lampshades are made from camel hides, which are then colored and decorated and finally plated with thin gold leaf.

Papier mâché

In Kashmir, in northern India, people make beautifully decorated trays, boxes, and other small objects from papier mâché. First, the objects are molded from a mixture of wet paper and glue. Then, they are covered all over with painted designs of flowers, birds, and animals. The fine details are painted using a single goat's hair. Finally, a layer of varnish is applied, making the objects stronger and giving them an attractive, shiny surface.

Carpets

Carpets and rugs are made in many areas of India, but the most famous are the intricately patterned carpets of Kashmir. The Kashmiri weavers make their carpets on a loom, knotting all the threads by hand. The weavers always leave a single, deliberate mistake in their weaving. This is done as a mark of respect to Allah (Muslims' god), because **Muslims** believe that only he is capable of perfection.

Toys and puppets

In many parts of India, wood-carvers make toys, dolls, and puppets. Usually, carvers follow traditional designs for animals and people, but they also create models of modern objects such as planes and cars. The toys and dolls are painted in vivid colors and are often decorated with fabric.

Street art

The cities of the Indian subcontinent are full of color. Gigantic posters for the latest films line the streets. Trucks, vans, and buses are often covered with hand-painted decorations, while rickshaws (open-air taxis pedaled by a driver) may have colorful fabric hoods with ribbons and ornaments hanging from them. During religious festivals in Rajasthan, carts with embroidered **canopies** are pulled through the streets.

In Old Delhi, a chaotic variety of street signs compete with an enormous movie poster for people's attention.

47

Cross-Currents

Over the course of India's long history, many different peoples arrived in the country and left their mark on its art and culture. At the same time, Indian arts and crafts have had a dramatic impact on the rest of the world.

The impact of the Arabs

The people with the strongest influence on Indian art were the **Arabs.** From the 700s onward, **Muslim** Arabs from the north began to arrive in India, bringing a new religion, new styles of building, and a different way of life. The **Mughals**, who ruled most of India from the 16th to the 19th century, were tolerant and curious about other religions. Mughal artists created artwork illustrating **Hindu** themes. They blended **Islamic** Persian styles with traditional Indian art forms.

British influences

By the 1750s British traders were controlling most of India, and in 1858 India became part of the British Empire. Western-style buildings were built all over the country, and British families brought Western-style paintings, ceramics, and fabrics from home. Many Indians adopted European dress.

During the **Raj,** many Indian artists and craftspeople produced works for Western tastes. Textile makers wove cloth with Western designs of flowers, and they embroidered tablecloths and handkerchiefs. Metalworkers made silver urns and plates and European-style jewelry. Indian furniture makers, also influenced by Western designs, created delicate chairs and cabinets.

During the Raj, many Indians adopted Western dress. In this photograph of the Nehru family, only the mother wears traditional Indian dress. The young boy, Jawaharlal Nehru, grew up to be India's first prime minister.

Indian influences

While Indian artists and craftspeople were being influenced by Western tastes, Indian decorative arts and architecture were having an impact in Europe. In 1851 the Great Exhibition was held in London. The exhibition, intended as a showcase for the best design in the world, included a splendid Indian court that was filled with examples of Indian crafts. In 1875 the department store Liberty and Company opened its "Oriental Galleries" in London, selling Indian fabrics and ornaments. The galleries were such a success that in 1890 the company opened a second branch in Paris.

48

The Brighton Pavilion was built in southern England in 1782. It was rebuilt from 1815 to 1823 by architect John Nash, at a time when the British presence in India was becoming more dominant. The building's "Oriental" style was heavily influenced by the Mughal palaces of India.

By the 1900s Indian styles of fabric design and interior decoration had become popular in the fashionable capitals of Europe and the United States. **Inlaid** metal vases, known as *bidri,* and inlaid wooden cabinets were especially prized. Women wore embroidered shawls from Kashmir and had decorated cushions and hangings in their homes. A group of artists, now known as the "Orientalists," painted exotic scenes of the East, and architects designed buildings with domes and delicate towers based on Mughal palaces.

49

Changes in painting

During the British **Raj**, many Indian artists were attracted to European styles of painting and began to produce landscapes and portraits, subjects that had never been part of the Indian artistic tradition. Painters experimented with watercolors and oil paints and started to show their subjects in a much more realistic way. By the end of the 19th century, many artists in India were producing paintings that showed Indian people and landscapes in a Western, **Victorian** style.

The Bengal School

However, not all Indian artists were happy with this new development, and during the 1890s a group of young Indian artists tried to get back in touch with their own traditions. One of the leaders of this group, which became known as the Bengal School, was Abanindranath Tagore. Influenced by Japanese art as well as by Mughal paintings and **Hindu** statues, he aimed to create a new kind of "Oriental art." Many of the Bengal School painters were involved in the struggle for Indian independence, which was finally achieved in 1947. Their paintings show noble, spiritual figures suffering under the burden of foreign rule.

This strikingly simple portrait of a woman was painted about 1900 by Abanindranath Tagore, one of the founding members of the Bengal School.

The early 20th century

In the 1920s many Indian artists began to experiment with contemporary Western styles. In particular, Gaganendranath Tagore was influenced by the **geometric** shapes of **Cubism,** creating magical paintings that played with ideas of light and pattern. Rabindranath Tagore used a **Surrealist** style for his masklike faces and monsters, which looked like creatures from ancient forests. Amrita Sher-Gil produced striking portraits of poor Indian women that resemble French artist Paul Gauguin's paintings of Tahitian women. Jamini Roy turned to ancient Indian scroll paintings for inspiration in his bold, simplified portraits.

Art after independence

In the same year that India became independent, a Progressive Artists' Group was set up in Bombay (later Mumbai). This group aimed to create modern art with a more worldwide appeal. Over the past 50 years, Indian art has become widely known around the world. Artists work in a range of styles and media, including sculpture and textile art, but their art is usually about India and its people, rather than being purely **abstract.** As India's leading modern artist, M. F. Husain, once said, "How can I go abstract when there are 600 million people around me in India?" Husain felt that he could not separate himself from reality and should focus on real life in his art.

M. F. Husain is a leading contemporary artist who depicts traditional subjects using both Indian and Western techniques. Here, his prancing horse is painted in a Cubist style.

◈ Indian style

Indian fabrics, cushions, and hangings became very popular in the West during the 1970s, when many young people traveled to India. Since then, Indian art has never really lost its popularity in the West. Indian fabrics, patterns, and colors inspire many contemporary fashion and interior designers.

51

Further Resources

Further reading

Chatterjee, Manini, and Roy, Anita. *Eyewitness Guides: India.* New York: Dorling Kindersley, 2002.

Dalal, Anita. *Nations of the World: India.* Chicago: Raintree, 2003.

Kilgallon, Conor. *India and Sri Lanka: Culture and Costumes.* Broomall, Penn.: Mason Crest, 2002.

In general guidebooks to India often have good sections on Indian culture.

Websites

http://www.artindia.net/
A site on dance and other performing arts in India.

http://www.asia.si.edu/collections/himalayanHome.htm
Indian art collections in the Smithsonian Museum, Washington, D.C.

http://jigyasa0.tripod.com/
A general site of Indian art, architecture, and history, with links to museums with Indian art collections and to essays on topics related to Indian art.

http://www.roamin-about.com/caves.html
Sculpture and paintings from the caves at Ajanta and Ellora.

http://www.taj-mahal.net/
A site that offers a virtual tour of the Taj Mahal.

Places to visit

United States

Cleveland Museum of Art, Ohio

Harvard University Art Museums, Cambridge, Massachusetts

Kimball Art Museum, Fort Worth, Texas

Los Angeles County Museum of Art, California

Metropolitan Museum of Art, New York

Minneapolis Institute of Arts, Minnesota

Museum of Fine Arts, Boston, Massachusetts

Philadelphia Museum of Art, Pennsylvania

San Diego Museum of Art, California

Canada

Royal Ontario Museum, Toronto

Canadian Museum of Civilization, Hull, Quebec

Glossary

abstract art that does not try to be realistic

appliqué technique of stitching cutout designs onto a larger piece of cloth

Arabs name given to people who live in the Middle East and North Africa. Most Arabs follow the religion of Islam.

Aryans tribes of people who arrived in India about 1500 B.C.E. The Aryans were the first Hindus.

bidri metalwork inlaid with colored enamel

Buddhism religion based on the teachings of the Buddha and practiced mainly in Eastern and Central Asia. Buddhists believe that you should not become too attached to material things and that you live many lives in different bodies.

canopy small roof or covering made from fabric

capital top or base of a pillar that is often decorated with carvings

Cubism early 20th-century art movement that represented objects in a fragmented, geometric way

earthenware pots or plates made from baked clay fired at a low temperature

enamel shiny, glasslike substance that is often inlaid in metal

engrave to cut a design or letters into a surface

epic long poem or story about heroic adventures or great battles

filigree delicate metalwork made from twisted wire

fire to heat clay up to a very high temperature to turn it into pottery

fresco painting on a wall or a ceiling done while the plaster is still wet

fretwork decorative carving including open spaces or relief

geometric featuring regular shapes, such as triangles, squares, and circles

glaze substance that is applied to pottery in the process of firing to create a shiny and/or colorful surface

Hinduism main religion of India. Hindus have many gods and believe that they live many lives in different bodies.

Hindustani music type of classical Indian music practiced in the north of the country

inlaid set into the surface of something

Islam religion based on the teachings of Muhammad. Muslims believe that Allah is God and that Muhammad is his prophet. Their religion is based on prayer, fasting, charity, and pilgrimage.

Jainism religion practiced mainly in India. Jains worship many gods and believe that all violence is wrong and that all forms of life are sacred.

Karnataka music type of classical Indian music practiced in the south of the country (from the region Karnataka)

kiln very hot oven where pottery is fired

lacquer to apply a substance that, when it dries, becomes a shiny, hard, protective coat

latticework form of art made by creating a framework of crossed wood or metal strips

Mahabharata long Hindu poem written down about 300 B.C.E. that tells the story of two rival families

maharaja Indian prince

meditation deep relaxation of the mind

minaret tall, slender tower of a mosque. Minarets often have a balcony from which Muslims are called to prayer.

mineral substance found in the earth

mosaic form of surface decoration made by inlaying small pieces of colored material, such as glass, to form an image or pattern

mosque building used by Muslims for worship

Mughals Muslim emperors who ruled most of India from 1526 to 1857

mural decoration that is painted or carved onto a wall

Muslim someone who follows the religion of Islam

nirvana a complete state of contentment and bliss

ocher color made from certain soils and used for painting or dyeing

pashmina shawl made from fine goat's wool

peninsula piece of land that juts out into the sea and is surrounded on three sides by water

pigment substance that gives color to something

pilgrimage religious journey to a holy place

Raj period when the British ruled India

Ramayana long Hindu poem written down between the 2nd and 4th centuries B.C.E. that tells the story of the Hindu god Rama and his wife Sita

relief carving that stands out from a surface

sanctuary especially holy place in a temple or other religious building

sari long piece of light material worn draped around the body. Saris are traditionally worn by Indian women and girls.

shrine holy building, smaller than a temple, that often includes statues or other holy objects

Sikhism form of religion practiced by some Indians, especially in the Punjab, in northwest India. Sikhs believe in a single god who created the universe, and that all humans are equal.

sitar Indian stringed musical instrument with a long neck

slip kind of semiliquid clay used like paint for decorating pots

stupa stone or brick dome that contains holy objects. Stupas are built by Buddhists and Jains.

stylized not realistic

Surrealism 20th-century art movement in which artists created dreamlike images

trappings saddles, reins, and bridles worn by animals

trellis frame of latticework used as a screen or as a wall for climbing plants

Victorian dating from the period when British Queen Victoria reigned, 1837–1901

votive offerings gifts offered to a god to ask for a favor or to give thanks for a blessing

Index